[Cov]er by Dugan Design Group

[Publ]ished in association with The Christopher Ferebee Agency

[52 WE]EKS THROUGH THE BIBLE DEVOTIONAL
[Copyri]ght © 2017 James Merritt
[Publishe]d by Harvest House Publishers
[Eugene,] Oregon 97402
[www.Har]vesthousepublishers.com

[ISBN 978]-0-7369-6562-0 (Milano Softone™)
[ISBN 978]-0-7369-6563-7 (eBook)

[Printed in C]hina

[20] 20 21 22 23 24 25 / RDS-SK / 10 9 8 7 6 5 4 3 2 1

52 WEEKS
THROUGH
THE BIBL
DEVOTION

JAME
MERRI

HARVEST HO
EUGE

V
H
Ty
Co
Pub

52 WE
Copyri
Publishe
Eugene,
www.har

ISBN 978
ISBN 978

Contents

Section Four: Gone But Not Forgotten

Section Five: One Solitary Life

Section Six: Church Matters

Section Seven: Curtain Call

Your 52 Weeks with the Bible

nside every Testament distributed by The Gideons International one will find this introduction:

> The Bible contains the mind of God, the state of man, the way of salvation, the doom of sinners, and the happiness of believers. Its doctrines are holy, its precepts are binding, its histories are true, and its decisions are immutable.
>
> Read it to be wise, believe it to be safe, and practice it to be holy. It contains light to direct you, food to support you, and comfort to cheer you.
>
> It is the traveler's map, the pilgrim's staff, the pilot's compass, the soldier's sword, and the Christian's charter. Here too, Heaven is opened and the gates of Hell disclosed.
>
> Christ is its grand subject, our good its

design, and the glory of God its end. It should fill the memory, rule the heart, and guide the feet. Read it slowly, frequently and prayerfully. It is a mine of wealth, a paradise of glory, and a river of pleasure.

It is given you in life, will be opened at the judgment, and be remembered forever. It involves the highest responsibility, rewards the greatest labor, and will condemn all who trifle with its sacred contents.[1]

I couldn't have said it better myself! Just as there is nobody like Jesus, there is no book like the Bible. Nothing has been more important to my walk with God, my role as a pastor, or my life as a Christian than reading God's word daily. My prayer as you read *52 Weeks Through the Bible Devotional* is that your appetite would be whetted to feed from the meat of God's word daily. It is the only book in the world that will satisfy you and leave you hungry for more at the same time!

Section One

Like No Other

‒‒‒‒

Even the most jaded critic of the Bible cannot deny the impact of this magnificent book on our culture, our nation, our world, and history itself. Its truths and teachings led to two of the greatest social movements in history—the abolition of lawful slavery throughout the Western Hemisphere and most other countries and the American Civil Rights Movement.[2] What the Bible has done for the world, it can do for your life. Read and be changed.

52 Weeks Through the Bible

1

Let's Take It from the Beginning

Then God said, "Let us make man in our image,
after our likeness. And let them have dominion over
the fish of the sea and over the birds of the heavens
and over the livestock and over all the earth and
over every creeping thing that creeps on the earth."
So God created man in his own image,
in the image of God he created him;
male and female he created them (GENESIS 1:26-27).

The word for *image* comes from a root that refers to a carving. We were carved into the shape of God to reflect him. That is not true of anything else in the universe.

No other created being has a mind to know God, a heart to love God, or a will to obey God. We are different mentally, morally, and spiritually. Only humans can have a relationship with God, and God only has a personal relationship with humans.

The heavens may declare the glory of God; the moon, the stars, and the planets may reveal the greatness of

God; the mountains and the oceans may show us the beauty of God, but only humans reflect the image of God. Plants have a body, animals have a body and soul, but only humans have a body, a soul, and a spirit. That spirit is part of the difference. The spirit is our reflection of the image of God.

52 Weeks Through the Bible

When we learn that mankind was created in God's image, we often think of it in the abstract: The great mass of humanity was created in the image of God. But what God wants us to grasp is the "personalness" of each of us being created in his image. *I* was created in his image. *You* were created in his image. The greatness of this realization, when personalized, is life-changing. It's also the place every Christian needs to start when they think of their assignment here on earth. Each of us was carved by God for two reasons: the first and foremost is that we might know, love, and obey God. He desires fellowship with each of us. The second reason is that we each have a calling while we're here on earth. Finding our calling begins with seeing how God has carved us. In what ways are we created to serve him best?

The greatness of these two reasons for our being created in God's image can motivate us for our entire life. We can never grow tired of knowing, loving, and obeying God. And when we enter into our calling, we can find lasting happiness working in God's vineyard using our unique talents.

Image - Carved into the shape of God, & to reflect him.

likeness - similar

dominion - rule/power

created - make

2

Paradise Lost

*The serpent was more crafty than any other beast
of the field that the LORD God had made.
He said to the woman, "Did God actually say, 'You
shall not eat of any tree in the garden'?" And the
woman said to the serpent, "We may eat of the fruit
of the trees in the garden, but God said, 'You shall
not eat of the fruit of the tree that is in the midst
of the garden, neither shall you touch it, lest you
die.'" But the serpent said to the woman, "You will
not surely die. For God knows that when you eat
of it your eyes will be opened, and you will be like
God, knowing good and evil"* (GENESIS 3:1-5).

Adam and Eve knew nothing of crime, murder, road
rage, war, credit-card debt, or sickness. Everything was
coming up roses when the first question ever asked in
the Bible takes place in Genesis 3:1: "Did God actually say, 'You shall not eat of any tree in the garden'?"

The serpent, otherwise known as "the devil" or
"Satan," crafted his question to make Eve question

God: "Did God actually say, 'You shall not eat of any tree in the garden'?" The answer was no. God said eat from *every* tree except the tree of the knowledge of good and evil.

The devil is never looking out for your best interests. Anytime he tells you to do something, he is not trying to help you; he is trying to hurt you. He will try to get you to doubt the word of God, and he will lie in the process.

52 Weeks Through the Bible

Satan was crafty in the garden. He knew that casting doubt on what God had said would enable him to present a temptation to Eve she couldn't resist. The story of human history is replete with Satan's crafty designs to cause men and women to doubt God and his word. The sad results have been predictable.

The apostle Paul reminded the Christians in Corinth that "we are not ignorant of [Satan's] designs" (2 Corinthians 2:11). Would that Eve could have said the same thing.

Satan is still crafty today. He knows my weaknesses and he knows yours. His first step in exploiting those weaknesses is to cast doubt on God, his word, and his care for us. When you read God's word, read it through believing eyes. Trust God and his word. Deny your enemy the foothold that will bring only destruction to your life.

crafty –
clever at achieving
one's aims by (indirect
or deceitful methods.

3

To the Rescue

You, who were dead in your trespasses and
the uncircumcision of your flesh, God made
alive together with him, having forgiven us
all our trespasses (COLOSSIANS 2:13).

There's the magic word—*forgiven*. That word contains the only antidote to the poison of sin that flows through our soul...

The word *forgiveness* means to "separate." Every one of us carries our sin with us like a ball and chain. We need someone to separate that sin from us. That is what God did at the cross of Jesus Christ...

How many of our sins were still out in the future when Jesus died? All of them. God had already factored in our sins and included them in Christ's death. We can know we've always been forgiven and are right with God because God has forgiven all of our sins—past, present, and future.

52 Weeks Through the Bible

Make no mistake about it—we were *all* dead in our trespasses before God, in his mercy, redeemed us by canceling our debt, nailing it to Christ's cross. The good news of the gospel is that all our many sins were paid for by the death of Christ. He was the sacrifice for our sins—past, present, and, yes, future. How free, then, are we from the penalty of sin? *Totally* free. One of our greatest defeats over Satan's schemes is precisely this: He can lay no charge against us that has not been answered by the cross of Christ. The cross utterly silences Satan's accusations against us. Thus we never need be cowed or shamed again. This is the great victory Christ won for us.

4

Happily Ever After

Then I saw a new heaven and a new earth, for the first heaven and the first earth had passed away, and the sea was no more. And I saw the holy city, new Jerusalem, coming down out of heaven from God, prepared as a bride adorned for her husband. And I heard a loud voice from the throne saying, "Behold, the dwelling place of God is with man. He will dwell with them, and they will be his people, and God himself will be with them as their God. He will wipe away every tear from their eyes, and death shall be no more, neither shall there be mourning, nor crying, nor pain anymore, for the former things have passed away" (Revelation 21:1-5).

For the first time, all of God's people will live in God's perfect presence. Our eyes will see him. Our ears will hear him. Our hands can touch him. Our lips can kiss him. He will never be out of sight. He will never be out of mind. He will be as he has always been, "God with us."

52 Weeks Through the Bible

In Genesis, the first book of the Bible, we read about God's creation of man and the fellowship God and man enjoyed in the garden. We also read of the fall that severed the intimacy of that relationship. But in Revelation, the final book of the Bible, we read that the fellowship God intended for us all along will finally culminate in a new heaven and a new earth. There, the dwelling place of God will be with man. He will dwell with us, and we will be his people. He will wipe every tear from our eyes, and there will be no more death, mourning, crying, or pain.

This, beloved believers, is what awaits us. This is our calling, our hope. In this future, orchestrated by God, we will dwell securely and contentedly for all eternity. During our pain-filled days here on earth, we can always turn our eyes to our future and once again place our trust in the one who knows us the best and loves us the most.

Section Two

A Nation Is Born

————

No nation has a more storied beginning than Israel. Visions and dreams lead to a race and a nation destined to become a blessing to the entire world. The story takes us from deserts to dungeons and from crossing parted seas to traversing deep rivers. A promised land is reached with divine miracles and life-changing messages littered along the way. Read and be changed.

52 Weeks Through the Bible

5

Yes, God

Does he who supplies the Spirit to you and works miracles among you do so by works of the law, or by hearing with faith—just as Abraham "believed God, and it was counted to him as righteousness"? Know then that it is those of faith who are the sons of Abraham. And the Scripture, foreseeing that God would justify the Gentiles by faith, preached the gospel beforehand to Abraham, saying, "In you shall all the nations be blessed." So then, those who are of faith are blessed along with Abraham, the man of faith (GALATIANS 3:5-9).

Do you know why we should always say yes to God? God wants to work through our yes to accomplish his best. When we say yes to God, we get blessed and we become a blessing.

Do you realize that every blessing in your life has come as a result of somebody saying yes? You are alive right now because your mother said yes to giving you life. You enjoy the freedom you have today because men and women said yes to defending this nation. You are alive today because God said yes to giving you another day. You can have eternal life when you say yes to Jesus Christ.

52 Weeks Through the Bible

———

Abraham said yes to God. The result was blessing upon blessing for Abraham and his descendants. And we who live today and believe in Christ are Abraham's descendants...not after the flesh, but after the spirit. When we said yes to God's invitation to forever fellowship with him, we became one of Abraham's spiritual kin. We have inherited blessing upon blessing, not just in this life, but in the life to come. Now that we're in the family of faith, God will still offer us many chances to say yes to his plan for our life. He can direct us to the right person to marry, the right vocation, the right ministry. In every circumstance that we surrender to God by saying yes, we can only find blessing. This too is part of our godly inheritance.

6

In the Crosshairs

His brothers then came and threw themselves down before him. "We are your slaves," they said. But Joseph said to them, "Don't be afraid. Am I in the place of God? You intended to harm me, but God intended it for good to accomplish what is now being done, the saving of many lives. So then, don't be afraid. I will provide for you and your children." And he reassured them and spoke kindly to them (Genesis 50:18-21 niv).

⟶———⟶

God isn't caught off guard when things go wrong in your life. He isn't surprised the way that you are. Not only is everything that happens in your life going according to God's plan, but it is going to accomplish his purpose.

You may need to be patient. It took Joseph a couple of decades to understand God's purpose, but here's what he discerned: "God sent me ahead of you to preserve for you a remnant on earth and to save your lives by a great deliverance" (Genesis 45:7 niv).

God's purpose was to save their lives, the lives of the ones who had harmed him. But that's not all. Joseph said, "God intended it for good to accomplish what is now being done, the saving of many lives" (Genesis 50:20 NIV). God's purpose was to save many lives.

When Joseph was sold into slavery in Egypt, he didn't know that one day a famine would come that could destroy the entire nation. He didn't know that he'd be placed in a powerful position to help save that nation. Joseph didn't know that in a hard confrontation, he'd preserve his family so that the nation of Israel could be born and the world could have a Savior. God doesn't love your hardship, but God does love life with his people and works his purpose so that we all can have it.

If you understand that God takes both the good and the bad, both friends and enemies, both fairness and unfairness to accomplish his purpose in your life, then you cannot be bitter. Joseph doesn't respond out of bitterness. Joseph doesn't impart more fear. He laid aside thoughts of revenge and put his brothers' fear to an end. "Don't be afraid. I'm not God."

52 Weeks Through the Bible

Every one of us have had events in our past when we wondered, *Where is God?* Sometimes—maybe weeks, months, or even years later—we find out why it happened. Sometimes we never find out why. In all cases, like Joseph, even when in our darkest dungeon, when every fiber of our being cries out, "Why, God?" we must trust that the end result will work to God's glory. Someone has wisely said, "Everything will turn out all right in the end. If it's not all right now, then it's not the end."

People often refer to the "patience of Job," but perhaps a better biblical model would be to have the patience of Joseph. If you're in the dark dungeon now and God has not revealed the *why* of the situation, you will simply have to trust. Trusting God patiently is never the wrong choice.

7

The Way to Freedom

The LORD said to Moses and Aaron in Egypt, "This month is to be for you the first month, the first month of your year. Tell the whole community of Israel that on the tenth day of this month each man is to take a lamb for his family, one for each household… The animals you choose must be year-old males without defect, and you may take them from the sheep or the goats. Take care of them until the fourteenth day of the month, when all the members of the community of Israel must slaughter them at twilight. Then they are to take some of the blood and put it on the sides and tops of the doorframes of the houses where they eat the lambs…Eat it in haste; it is the LORD's Passover. "On that same night I will pass through Egypt and strike down every firstborn of both people and animals, and I will bring judgment on all the gods of Egypt. I am the LORD. The blood will be a sign for you on the houses where you are, and when I see the blood, I will pass over you. No destructive plague will touch you when I strike Egypt.

"This is a day you are to commemorate; for the generations to come you shall celebrate it as a festival to the LORD—a lasting ordinance" (EXODUS 12:1-14 NIV).

When God frees you from whatever is binding you, a new day dawns and a new life emerges. Passover marked a new beginning for these Jewish people and bound them together as one nation under God. From then until now, every time Jewish believers would hear the words *redeem* or *redemption*, they would think of the Passover. God had delivered them through the blood of the lamb, and he delivers us the same way today.

Do you remember how the lamb had to be perfect? How every part of that lamb had to be examined over a period of time to make sure there was no blot or blemish? Jesus Christ, the Lamb of God, was examined for thirty years. The Sadducees, Pharisees, Herodians, and synagogue leaders all posed hard questions to Jesus. Even Pontius Pilate examined him and concluded, "I find no fault in him." Jesus was *the* perfect Lamb.

When you study the Passover you are not just looking into a window of what God did then. You are looking into a mirror of what God is doing today. They were saved by the blood of a lamb—not a single Hebrew home lost a child—and we are saved in the same way.

Every one of us was born with sin over the door-post of our heart. Once we place our faith in Jesus, our sins disappear. When God looks at your heart, he either sees your sins or Jesus's blood. The only way to freedom and to eternal life is by the blood of God's Lamb.

52 Weeks Through the Bible

———

When you became a Christian, you became a partaker of the security available through the blood of Christ. It's as if the blood of the spotless Lamb was applied to the doorposts of your life, just as it was to the doorposts of the Hebrew homes on that unforgettable first Passover night.

The blood will remain as the security against your sin for all eternity. Through that blood, you are reckoned by God as innocent as the slain Lamb. Whenever Satan tries to remind you of your past sins, simply point him to the blood of the Lamb applied for you. Against the blood of Christ, Satan has no argument.

8

Catch-22

Moses answered the people, "Do not be afraid. Stand firm and you will see the deliverance the LORD will bring you today. The Egyptians you see today you will never see again. The LORD will fight for you; you need only to be still" (Exodus 14:13-14 NIV).

The children of Israel have just escaped from 430 years of slavery. They have followed God out of Egypt and are painfully aware that this decision has led them into a corner. This wasn't a navigational error. They hadn't miscalculated or taken a wrong turn. God had led them to this dead end. God will do that so we will learn to trust him and follow his ways. We never quit learning to trust him.

The bad news is that God will lead us to Red Seas, but the good news is that God goes with us and before us. Begin every day signing a Declaration of Dependence upon God because if he leads you that day to a place of desperation and despair, you will stay there until it becomes a place of complete dependence on

him. Depend upon God not only to lead you wherever he wants you to go, but also to make a way out
once you get there.

52 Weeks Through the Bible

━━▸━▸━▸━

When backed into a corner, our first reaction
is to fight. We look for our earthly weapons
and prepare to make our way out of the dead-
end situation we're in. But what did God tell the children of Israel? Did he say to be fearful? Did he give a
call to action on their part? Did he tell them to take up
their swords for battle? There were times later on when
God would indeed equip them for battle, but not here.
Instead, now was a time when they were to reject fear,
stand firm, and then see with their own eyes the deliverance of the Lord.

God often allows us to fall into perilous situations to
invite us to see, with our own eyes, his power to deliver
us. What a difference it would make if we could face
every impending dark situation by standing still, totally
unafraid, and watching the Lord bring deliverance on
our behalf.

9

The Need to Succeed

Moses my servant is dead. Now therefore arise, go over this Jordan, you and all this people, into the land that I am giving to them, to the people of Israel. Every place that the sole of your foot will tread upon I have given to you, just as I promised to Moses. From the wilderness and this Lebanon as far as the great river, the river Euphrates, all the land of the Hittites to the Great Sea toward the going down of the sun shall be your territory. No man shall be able to stand before you all the days of your life. Just as I was with Moses, so I will be with you. I will not leave you or forsake you. Be strong and courageous, for you shall cause this people to inherit the land that I swore to their fathers to give them. Only be strong and very courageous, being careful to do according to all the law that Moses my servant commanded you. Do not turn from it to the right hand or to the left, that you may have good success wherever you go. This Book of the Law shall not depart from your mouth, but you shall meditate on it day and night, so that you may be careful to do according to all that is written in it. For then you will make your way prosperous, and then you will have good success. Have I not commanded you? Be strong and courageous. Do

not be frightened, and do not be dismayed, for the LORD
your God is with you wherever you go (JOSHUA 1:2-9).

———

God guarantees to fulfill only his purpose for your
life. We don't create our purpose; we discover and
pursue it. Joshua knew he had nailed it; he had the
presence of God, he obeyed the principles of God,
and he was filled with the purpose of God. Success
was guaranteed.

Just look at the way God brought Joshua from an
unlikely success to an irresistible success. He didn't do
it in a human way, picking and choosing what works
based on studies and surveys. He did it God's way.

Listen again to what God said to Joshua in verse 5:
"No man shall be able to stand before you all the days
of your life. Just as I was with Moses, so I will be with
you. I will not leave you or forsake you."

Did you hear what God said to him? God said, "If
you will recognize my presence, obey my will, and
fulfill the purpose I have put you on this planet to
fulfill, *no one will stand against you.* You will be an
irresistible force, an immovable object. Every foe you
meet will be the foe you beat." Nothing and no one
can stand against anyone who stands with God.

The Bible is not about your personal fulfillment, accomplishments, or happiness. The Bible is about God's presence with you, how you fit into his plan, and how you can be fulfilled through his purposes, not your own. God will feed your need for success with the only success that matters—his.

We were put on this earth to experience the presence of God, obey the principles of God, and fulfill the purpose of God. When we do, success is guaranteed.

52 Weeks Through the Bible

———••◦••———

Each of us has the promise of God's presence as we, by faith, claim the "land" that is ours. Yes, we each have a calling and a place in the work of God. As we move into that sacred place—that promised land—we can know that no matter what adversity comes against us, no man (or messenger from Satan) will be able to stand before us. As God was with Moses, so he promised to be with Joshua—and through faith, with us also. He will never leave us nor forsake us. This is his promise—and it's by this promise that we're able to dwell successfully in our calling.

Out on a Limb

In those days Israel had no king;
everyone did as they saw fit
(JUDGES 21:25 NIV).

⇥⇥⇥

God is necessary for true morality. Rightness and wrongness is founded on God, and only with God can we know that evil and wrong will be punished and goodness and righteousness will be rewarded. With God we know that the scales of justice will be balanced.

Suppose you could have morality without God. What good is morality without accountability? If no afterlife exists, what difference does it make whether you live like Mother Teresa or Adolf Hitler? Without God, those rapists got away with it. Those who were guilty of genocide got away with it. Without God, militant terrorists, crooked politicians, and religious hypocrites all get away with it.

Without God, you are out on a moral limb. Jesus defines and declares right and wrong from the cross.

The wrong is what he died for so that we could be made right. He alone decides which is which. When we look to Jesus and live by his word, we will not only know what is right, we will do what is right in the only eyes that matter—the God whose compass is love.

52 Weeks Through the Bible

W hat a different world this would be if everyone simply did the right thing every time. What if every person did what was best for his or her neighbor, even if it was inconvenient? True morality comes from God. Doing the right thing is doing the God-like thing. Doing what is right in our own eyes is the human, fleshly, and deadly choice.

Someday the scales of justice will balance, and all will be called into account. But until that day, we have the opportunity to make the world better and to be a vibrant witness to the God whose divine morality we reflect to others. Let us always do what is right, not in our own eyes, but in God's eyes.

11

The Beauty of Suffering

Then Job replied to the Lord:
"I know that you can do all things;
no purpose of yours can be thwarted.
You asked, 'Who is this that obscures
my plans without knowledge?'
Surely I spoke of things I did not understand,
things too wonderful for me to know.
"You said, 'Listen now, and I will speak;
I will question you,
and you shall answer me.'
My ears had heard of you
but now my eyes have seen you.
Therefore I despise myself
and repent in dust and ashes"
(Job 42:1-6 niv).

In Job 42:2-3, Job acknowledges three things about God:

1. God controls this universe and nothing can frustrate his eternal purposes.

2. Everything has a divine purpose. Not one molecule in this universe is without a design.

3. We don't always understand God.

You never have to *understand* what God is doing if you can *trust* God to control rightly. When you are going through adversity and pain and suffering that you don't understand, knowing all the answers is less important than knowing the One who does.[3]

God not only gives us the good, he also allows us to suffer the bad. This is because God is interested in our holiness and in his glory before he's ever interested in our happiness. Our own wisdom can't reconcile this, but the promise implies a purpose.

If we can accept that God is more interested in our holiness than our happiness, then we can begin to accept that God's grace, not our suffering, is the point.

52 Weeks Through the Bible

＞━━━＞

Accepting God's sovereignty is easy when we're enjoying his blessings. But when tragedy strikes, when unexpected reversals come our way, or when we receive a troubling diagnosis, we tend to question God. Why us? Why now? And yet as Christians we must be content to let God be God. As the saying goes, when we can't see God's hand, we must trust his heart. And his heart is always toward his people.

Section Three

Wise Kings

———————

God gave Israel the two greatest kings who ever lived—David and Solomon. One was a champion of warfare, the other a champion of wisdom. Together this father-son combo takes us far beyond the political side of royalty to the spiritual side of life. By practice and precept, they offer a glimpse into how to make wise choices in the journey of life. Read and be changed.

52 Weeks Through the Bible

How to Say Yes to the Giant

*David said to Saul, "Your servant used to keep
sheep for his father. And when there came a lion,
or a bear, and took a lamb from the flock, I went
after him and struck him and delivered it out of
his mouth. And if he arose against me, I caught
him by his beard and struck him and killed him.
Your servant has struck down both lions and
bears, and this uncircumcised Philistine shall be
like one of them, for he has defied the armies of
the living God... The* Lord *who delivered me
from the paw of the lion and from the paw of
the bear will deliver me from the hand of this
Philistine." And Saul said to David, "Go, and
the* Lord *be with you!"* (1 Samuel 17:34-37).

David could face the fearful present because of what
he remembered from a frightening past. He recalled
how with nothing more than a staff, a slingshot, and
his bare hands, he had killed a bear and a lion by the
power of God.

Do you know why we fear our giants? We forget what we ought to remember and we remember what we ought to forget. We tend to remember our failures and forget our victories. We tend to remember our low points and forget our high points.

If you remember what God has done for you, you will trust what God will do for you. But if you forget what God has done for you, you will doubt what God will do for you.

Hindsight gives a lot of insight, and David said to Saul, "God has a perfect track record. He always comes through. He never fails. God can give me victory today because he gave me victory yesterday. He is no different today than he was yesterday."

52 Weeks Through the Bible

W hat are your giants? Name them, one by one. Then remember that the God who empowered David to strike down his giant is the same God who will be with you as you contend with the seemingly insurmountable giants stalking you. Here is a time to remember how God has intervened in the past and to look forward to what he will do in your present situation.

It's time to have faith in the God who causes his chosen ones to win against giants, even with the weakest of tools. No, it wasn't the slingshot that slayed the giant. It was the God of David who gave the victory. He is your God too.

13

Just the Two of Us

*Delight yourself in the LORD, and he will give
you the desires of your heart* (PSALM 37:4).

Just as a husband and wife need time together, all
intimate relationships—friends, parents and their
children—benefit from one-on-one time. We also
need time together with our Father in heaven. We
need to bathe him in loving worship while he wraps
us in love. Call it whatever you want—a quiet time,
a devotional life—we need that time alone with God.

God, too, desires this time with us. He wants us to
spend time with him so badly that he paid in order
to get it. He sent Jesus to remove every barrier, tear
down every wall, bridge every gulf, unlock every door
so that we could have a personal relationship with
him. Teresa and I got married because we couldn't
bear to live life apart. In the same way, God wants
us to have unrestricted access to him, anywhere and
anytime we want. God has a personal side, and he
wants us to know it.

52 Weeks Through the Bible

If we're like the average Christian, we can be prone to letting our relationship with God slide. In a good marriage, both partners need to communicate and experience intimacy often. So too with God, we must take time to enjoy intimate times of refreshing. God always shows up for a designated "quiet time." So must we if we desire deep intimacy with God. Remember, the most important appointment you have today is with God.

14

The Way to the Will

If any of you lacks wisdom, let him ask God,
who gives generously to all without reproach,
and it will be given him (JAMES 1:5).

What would you ask God for if he said to you, "Ask for whatever you want me to give you"? An egotistical person would ask for fame. A materialistic person would ask for wealth. An ambitious person would ask for power. A bitter person would ask for revenge. But listen to how Solomon responds to God's offer: "Give me wisdom and knowledge" (2 Chronicles 1:10 NIV).

The order that Solomon put those words is important. You can have a lot of knowledge and a little wisdom, but if you have a lot of wisdom, you have a lot of knowledge.

You can do what Solomon did. You can ask for something bigger than fame, wealth, power, or revenge. Anytime you want wisdom you can ask for it. About eight hundred years after Solomon's dream came true, the brother of Jesus wrote: "If any of you lacks wisdom, let him ask God, who gives generously to all without reproach, and it will be given him" (James 1:5).

You don't have to be a king to need wisdom and you don't have to be a king to ask for it. The same deal God made with Solomon he will make with you— "wisdom and knowledge will be given you."

Our problem is we have enough knowledge to make foolish decisions, but we don't have enough wisdom to make wise decisions. God doesn't give wisdom to the people who think they know it all. He gives it only to the person who admits he doesn't know enough.

52 Weeks Through the Bible

God is the dispenser of wisdom, and if we're brave enough to admit it, every one of us lacks the required wisdom to get through life successfully. But often we forget or simply refuse to ask God for wisdom. We survey a situation, and without so much as a whispered prayer for wisdom, we embark on a seemingly well-reasoned response. We rely on our available knowledge...but knowledge without wisdom solves nothing. God is not reluctant to give us wisdom. He is, in fact, waiting for us to simply ask and believe. All the wisdom necessary is just a prayer away.

15

Getting into Position

Trust in the LORD with all your heart,
and do not lean on your own understanding.
In all your ways acknowledge him,
and he will make straight your
paths (PROVERBS 3:5-6).

You are who you are, what you are, and where you are
in your life right now because of the choices you have
made: your major in college, the person you married,
your work, and where you live.

Every one of us would love to take back some decisions. We would all love do-overs. We golfers would
all like some mulligans. Others might wish for a
remodel or a makeover, an upgrade or a cure. Whatever you call it, God calls it redemption, and it's the
cry of every heart in our broken world.

52 Weeks Through the Bible

God has an uncanny way of making even our wrong decisions turn out right…if we trust in him with all our heart and don't lean on our own understanding. No matter where we are right now, we need to know by faith that God is active in our life and circumstances. The moment we submit our ways to him, we can see him begin to make our paths straight. That "wrong" decision you made? Yes, that too is redeemable. By faith, you will see God turn it into a profitable decision.

16

Difference Maker

Nobody remembers what happened yesterday.
And the things that will happen tomorrow?
Nobody'll remember them either.
Don't count on being remembered
(ECCLESIASTES 1:11 MSG).

What would life mean without God? If our lives are doomed to end in death, then not only does life not matter, it doesn't matter how we live. The scientist working in a lab trying to advance human knowledge, the doctor trying to find the cure for cancer to alleviate pain and suffering, the diplomat working overtime to promote peace in the world, and the soldier sacrificing to protect his country and keep people free participate, Solomon says, in work that means nothing without God.

Take a look at what gives you meaning. Add up all your title deeds, stocks and bonds, all the times you get your name in a newspaper, all your money, promotions, and achievements. Without God, it is one big zero.

52 Weeks Through the Bible

Our life has meaning...whether we see it now or not. But that meaning is often hidden from us as we go about our daily lives. It takes trust and faith to know that we're here for a divine purpose. And then it takes a willingness to discover our purpose and walk it out. Woe to those who go through life without ever discovering why they're here.

How do you find your purpose? Pray, pursue the interests God has given you, and look for opportunities to help others with their spiritual or temporal needs.

Gone But Not Forgotten

━━◆◆◆━━

Some of the greatest bearers of truth in history were God's prophets. In our day, when courage and conviction are lacking, these ancient prophetic messages are as fresh as daisies and still pulsate with practical principles and divine power. Read and be changed.

52 Weeks Through the Bible

17

Seeing Clearly

In the year that King Uzziah died, I saw the Lord,
high and exalted, seated on a throne; and the train of
his robe filled the temple. Above him were seraphim,
each with six wings: With two wings they covered their
faces, with two they covered their feet, and with two
they were flying. And they were calling to one another:
"Holy, holy, holy is the LORD Almighty;
the whole earth is full of his glory."
At the sound of their voices the
doorposts and thresholds shook
and the temple was filled with smoke.
"Woe to me!" I cried. "I am ruined! For I am a man of
unclean lips, and I live among a people of unclean lips,
and my eyes have seen the King, the LORD Almighty."
Then one of the seraphim flew to me with a live coal
in his hand, which he had taken with tongs from the
altar. With it he touched my mouth and said, "See,
this has touched your lips; your guilt is taken away
and your sin atoned for" (ISAIAH 6:1-7 NIV).

The God who created the universe wants to have a personal, eternal relationship with you. Many people don't have a relationship with God because the God they claim to have a relationship with is not God, just a functional image. When our relationship is not based on reality, our rapport is ruptured.

If your view of God is wrong, then your view of life is wrong. Your view of success is wrong. Your view of what is important is wrong. Even your view of yourself is wrong. We must see God the way God sees himself because having a real relationship with the real God is paramount. It does no good to get up close and personal with a God who is not real.

52 Weeks Through the Bible

───────

Seeing God as he really is causes us, like Isaiah the prophet, to be "ruined." We feel unclean amidst an unclean people. How can a holy God desire to have a relationship with men and women such as us? Yet the story of the Bible is just that. A holy God, high and exalted, seated on a throne with the train of his robe filling the temple, *wants* us as his very own. That this is the case seems impossible, but it is true. At such a revelation, we can only erupt in praise to our heavenly King.

18

Breaking the Prayer Barrier

This is what the LORD says, he who made the earth, the LORD who formed it and established it—the LORD is his name: "Call to me and I will answer you and tell you great and unsearchable things you do not know" (JEREMIAH 33:2-3 NIV).

In the spiritual world there is—at some point for all of us—another barrier that seems to be unbreakable. I call it the "prayer barrier." I've never been satisfied with my prayer life. It's hard for me. If you are like me, you would like to know how to consistently and constantly break the prayer barrier, because if what we believe is true, then the greatest source of untapped power in your life, my life, and in the entire church is wrapped up in prayer…

Maybe your big question is, "Does God always answer prayer?" The answer is yes. The only prayer that God doesn't answer is the prayer that is never prayed. Baptist evangelist F.B. Meyer once wrote,

"The great tragedy of life is not unanswered prayer: it is unoffered prayer."

52 Weeks Through the Bible

———

It's likely that most Christians experience a prayer barrier now and then. Maybe even frequently. Perhaps you're one of those Christians. I sure am. My mind wanders or I get sleepy or I feel like prayers never make it past the ceiling. When that happens, it helps for me to remember the power of the God to whom I'm praying. He is a prayer-answering God and he desires to hear me pray, to hear me cast my cares on him, to worship him as my Lord. His invitation is for us to call to him with the promise that he will answer and tell us great and unsearchable things we do not know. This is an invitation we refuse at our own peril.

19

The Devil in the Details

Be alert and of sober mind. Your enemy the devil prowls around like a roaring lion looking for someone to devour. Resist him, standing firm in the faith, because you know that the family of believers throughout the world is undergoing the same kind of sufferings (1 PETER 5:8-9 NIV).

You can ask any army general or head coach, "What is the greatest key to victory?" and both of them will tell you that the key is to know your opponent.

We know our opponents well, don't we? We know thieves are more likely to strike at night, so we lock our windows and install motion-sensor lights. We know that germs are the culprits of disease, and if we don't kill them first, they'll kill us. We know not to leave our purses in grocery carts, meet strangers in private places, or accept rides from strangers. We are well-versed in the ways and means of our everyday potential villains, and we live in defensive ways to protect ourselves.

How much more should we know an opponent who is out to ruin our lives, victimize our kids, and keep us away from God? Be assured that this is Satan's agenda, one he achieves by making sin look attractive. As the world's greatest salesman, he wants you to think he's leading you to safe places that will bring you happiness. We need to beware.

52 Weeks Through the Bible

To not acknowledge the existence of an enemy is the first major step to losing a war. And each of us *is* at war. We all have a despicable enemy who knows our weak points and looks for opportunities to exploit them. For that reason, we must be alert. But beyond just acknowledging our enemy and being alert, we must also steadfastly *resist* the overtures of the enemy by standing firmly in faith. Active (not passive) faith wins over Satan's designs on us. As we wage war by faith, we can see the enemy retreat as victory is ours. Do not let yourself be devoured through ignorance of the enemy's tactics.

20

A Line in the Sand

*Then the king ordered Ashpenaz, chief of his court
officials, to bring into the king's service some of the
Israelites from the royal family and the nobility—
young men without any physical defect, handsome,
showing aptitude for every kind of learning, well
informed, quick to understand, and qualified to
serve in the king's palace. He was to teach them the
language and literature of the Babylonians. The king
assigned them a daily amount of food and wine from
the king's table. They were to be trained for three years,
and after that they were to enter the king's service.
Among those who were chosen were some from Judah:
Daniel, Hananiah, Mishael and Azariah. The
chief official gave them new names: to Daniel, the
name Belteshazzar; to Hananiah, Shadrach; to
Mishael, Meshach; and to Azariah, Abednego.
But Daniel resolved that he would not defile
himself with the royal food and wine, and he
asked the chief official for permission not to
defile himself this way* (DANIEL 1:3-8 NIV).

In that Middle Eastern culture, when you sat down to eat a meal, particularly with a ruler or a king, it was a sign of a covenant commitment. You were pledging loyalty to the king, to submit to and share his life. But the only one Daniel was going to submit to was God, and he wanted to make that clear. Never cross a line that God has drawn. The world will tempt you, but when you stay on the God side, you will stay on the good side.

52 Weeks Through the Bible

———

Just as Daniel and his three friends were given food from the king's table—obviously very good food—so too are we given food from the table of this present world. Yes, it looks attractive. It tastes good too. Why then should we not partake?

We're told that Daniel, Shadrach, Meshach, and Abednego were "without defect." But the reason Daniel gave for not eating food from the king's table was that it would defile him. This attractive meal would do great harm to these men, and they were wise enough to abstain from what God had prohibited.

Each of us is in some way tempted to dine from the

king of this world's table. The fare looks delicious and will be pleasing to the taste…but to eat that which God has forbidden is to partake of poison.

What is it in your life that is being offered as food from the king's table? Have you already partaken and experienced its sad effects? If so, resolve now to push back your chair from the king's table and stay on the God side…the *good* side.

21

Take the Heat

*At that time certain Chaldeans came forward
and maliciously accused the Jews. They declared
to King Nebuchadnezzar, "O king, live forever!
You, O king, have made a decree, that every man
who hears the sound of the horn, pipe, lyre, trigon,
harp, bagpipe, and every kind of music, shall fall
down and worship the golden image. And whoever
does not fall down and worship shall be cast into
a burning fiery furnace. There are certain Jews
whom you have appointed over the affairs of the
province of Babylon: Shadrach, Meshach, and
Abednego. These men, O king, pay no attention to
you; they do not serve your gods or worship the golden
image that you have set up"* (DANIEL 3:8-12).

Nebuchadnezzar raised a ninety-foot golden image
of his pagan god. It must have been a tremendous
sight. Everybody who was a somebody had gathered
to join the cult of conformity. He had established a
new religious obligation, and at the appointed time

he wanted everyone to bow down and worship this new image.

Then the wind of this demonic commandment collides with the wall of a divine courage. Three young Hebrew men—Shadrach, Meshach, and Abednego—stood up when everybody else bowed down, and their actions were reported to the king. They were courageous rather than compromising.

You've heard it before and maybe you've *said* it before:

> "Well, I don't believe I ought to let my beliefs interfere with my politics."

> "When in Babylon do what the Babylonians do."

> "I don't believe I ought to impose my morality on someone else."

> "I'll bow down on the outside. I just won't bow down on the inside."

> "It is legal so I guess it must be right."

…One of the greatest lessons a parent will ever teach their child is to have the courage to stand for what is right even when they stand alone. The only place you will find this courage is in God. When you stand for what is right, you never stand alone. God always stands with you.

52 Weeks Through the Bible

What does a Christian do when their culture accepts what God rejects? For Shadrach, Meshach, and Abednego, the choice was obvious. They had to go with God's standards, not the culture's.

A lover of God will always choose the ways of God, even if it means the loss of friends or family, or possibly the end of a good job.

It's called *courage*, and it's the hallmark of every mature Christian. Each of us must ask ahead of time what we'll do when our culture is on a collision course with our faith. And we can take our cues from Shadrach, Meshach, and Abednego and teach our children to do likewise.

22

The Fugitive

In my distress I called to the LORD,
and he answered me.
From deep in the realm of the dead I called for help,
and you listened to my cry (JONAH 2:2 NIV).

━━━━

Jonah has been swallowed by a great fish and now, engulfed in total darkness and smelling the stench, he is alert to God. The belly of that fish was a rock-bottom experience, and when you are at the bottom, up is the only way you can look. For Jonah, a prophet, he looked "toward the temple," the place where he knew he would find God. If you are at a point where you don't know where to turn, you can always turn to God. You can always look up, and when you do, you will find God was there all the time...

Every day that you run from God is a wasted day. Don't waste any more. Look up, speak up, and give up; he will pick you up, not because you deserve it, but to teach you that he is a second-chance God.

52 Weeks Through the Bible

Like Jonah, we are often tempted to run from God's will for us. We're bombarded with "What ifs" or "Has God really said…?"

When God reveals his will for us, the only direction we can go is forward to embrace that calling. We can't let doubt or fear stand in the way of fulfilling our mission here on earth. Wasted days turn into wasted weeks, months, and years. Do we really want to look back on our life and see decades of a Jonah life? No, not when we grasp the love of God in bringing us to our calling… our Nineveh.

23

For Goodness' Sake

The fruit of the Spirit is love, joy, peace, patience, kindness, goodness, faithfulness, gentleness, self-control; against such things there is no law (GALATIANS 5:22-23).

⟫━━━

You may not know that the word *good* comes from an old Anglo-Saxon word that had the same connotation as *God*. *Good-bye* is an abbreviation of the saying, "God be with you." *Good* means "to be like God."

So it isn't surprising to see that *good* is listed as a trait of those who live according to the Holy Spirit…

As Christians, we believe that the Holy Spirit takes up residence in the lives of believers. The inclusion of goodness as a fruit of the Spirit tells us that God gives it. We cannot manufacture goodness.

Apart from God, no true goodness exists, and no one does good. Romans 3:12 says, "No one does good, not even one." But our potential for goodness is animated by the Spirit who lives in us, and with this fruit, he wants you and me to live in such a way that our lives will taste good to others.

52 Weeks Through the Bible

━━━━━

Fruit is made to be eaten so that it will nourish us. The fruit of God's Holy Spirit is to have a similar effect. We partake of the Holy Spirit as believers in Christ, and the divine fruit comes naturally to us—well, *super*naturally to us. As we display this fruit, we become witnesses to *good*. We become witnesses to God. Each and every day, we can allow God's Holy Spirit to reproduce his life in us. But it's crucial to realize that apart from him, we can produce nothing good.

Live the good life by living the God life.

24

On the Ropes

The righteous shall live by his faith (HABAKKUK 2:4).

Habakkuk was a prophet called by God who knew God but wrestled with God. He lived in the nation of Judah in a time of rebellion, idolatry, drunkenness, and wickedness. He had been praying and praying for God to bring repentance to his people and revival to his country. He never heard anything in response. Confused and frustrated, he confronted God: "You are supposed to be holy and righteous. Why don't you do something to punish your wicked people? Why don't you answer my prayer? What are you up to? Where are you right now?"

Then God answers: "I *am* going to do something. I am going to send the most wicked nation on the planet to crush my people." Habakkuk couldn't believe his ears. "This is your solution? No matter how wicked my people are, they are not as bad as the Babylonians. How could you, a holy and righteous God, do this?" To which God replies, "I know what I am doing, and I will do what is right. Trust me."

Then the Lord told Habakkuk to write down one of the greatest statements in all the Bible. It is a statement that sparked the Protestant Reformation. It is a statement that transformed the church: "The righteous shall live by his faith" (Habakkuk 2:4).

When we face tough times, we will take one of two paths: the path of fear, or the path of faith. If you are living in fear over anything that could end up in a bad way for your family, your finances, or your future, Habakkuk will show you that fear is defeated by focused faith.

52 Weeks Through the Bible

<hr />

Focused faith obviously implies something to focus *on*. For us as Christians, our faith is focused entirely on God. We've all learned by sad experience that turning our eyes away from God can only lead to sinking in the deep waters of life. Just ask Peter, who was able to walk on water as long as he focused on Christ. But when he turned his focus elsewhere—on the deep waters surrounding him—then he began to sink.

We live by faith. No matter what. No matter when. When we do this, we hear God say, "I will do what is right. Trust me."

25

On the Money

"Will man rob God? Yet you are robbing me. But you
say, 'How have we robbed you?' In your tithes and
contributions. You are cursed with a curse, for you
are robbing me, the whole nation of you. Bring the
full tithe into the storehouse, that there may be food
in my house. And thereby put me to the test, says
the LORD of hosts, if I will not open the windows of
heaven for you and pour down for you a blessing
until there is no more need. I will rebuke the devourer
for you, so that it will not destroy the fruits of your
soil, and your vine in the field shall not fail to bear,"
says the LORD of hosts (MALACHI 3:8-11).

You may think you earn your money by the good job
that you have or the good work that you do. However…it is God who gives life and health so you can
work. Being able to work doesn't ensure you a job, so
it is God who gives you the opportunity to have a
job and earn that paycheck. Everything that is repre-
sented by that paycheck comes from God: the abil-
ity, the knowledge, the health, the job, and the money.

King David desired to build a temple for the Lord. He took up an offering from the people to do so and they gave generously. They rejoiced and praised God for the financial victory. David prayed a beautiful prayer before these people and said, "But who am I, and who are my people, that we should be able to give as generously as this? Everything comes from you, and we have given you only what comes from your hand" (1 Chronicles 29:14 NIV).

The first key to learning how to handle money is to remember, *It's not your money. It is God's.*

52 Weeks Through the Bible

Counting one's blessings is not a new concept, but it's often one that's not practiced daily. Any wise Christian quickly learns that all he or she has comes from the hand of God. We may have a good job or have received a rich inheritance or worked hard to create our own successful business, but in every case, it was God behind the scenes bringing us our blessing. Not only bringing our blessing, but *sustaining* our blessing.

In short, we are always dependent on God, not on

our own resources. This is true during times of plenty and also during the lean times of life. Our response to God's blessings, be they large or small, is to give thanks and to return to God a significant portion for the work of his ministry.

Section Five

One Solitary Life

———▸▸▸▸———

The most important character in the book that changed everything is the one who changed everything—Jesus. His life is written in four Gospels that cover his last three years and is the major source of what we know about the most influential person by far who has ever lived. They explain why he should be trusted and worshiped. Read and be changed.

52 Weeks Through the Bible

26

Gospel Truth

*Inasmuch as many have undertaken to compile a
narrative of the things that have been accomplished
among us, just as those who from the beginning
were eyewitnesses and ministers of the word have
delivered them to us, it seemed good to me also,
having followed all things closely for some time past,
to write an orderly account for you, most excellent
Theophilus, that you may have certainty concerning
the things you have been taught* (LUKE 1:1-4).

Luke was writing for Theophilus, who was evidently
a new convert to Christianity and was beginning
to have doubts. Luke wanted him to know that he
had a firm foundation to believe what he had been
taught and to have certainty of the historical reality
of Jesus. More than a philosophical system, faith in
Jesus is built on the historical Jesus dying a historical death and experiencing a historical resurrection.
More than historical reliability, it is historical reality. Verified time and time again by the archeological

spade, Luke's Gospel continues to win over its harshest critics.

For Luke, the Christian faith is not a leap into the dark and a hope for the best. It is a rigorous faith that rests on the solid foundation of the most reliable facts. It initiates hope, instills trust, and inspires faith both in Luke's day and in ours.

52 Weeks Through the Bible

I t's important for every Christian to know their hope is built on the solid rock of evidence and not on the shifting sands of speculation. Your faith can survive attacks from the enemy or skeptical friends and family members because eyewitnesses like Matthew, Mark, Luke, and John accurately recorded what they saw. When your faith is assailed from within or without, take a lesson from Luke and know "that you may have certainty concerning the things you have been taught."

27

Don't Touch That Dial!

As he considered these things, behold, an
angel of the Lord appeared to him in a dream,
saying, "Joseph, son of David, do not fear
to take Mary as your wife, for that which is
conceived in her is from the Holy Spirit"
(MATTHEW 1:20).

God spoke to Joseph in an unusual space. God doesn't speak to Joseph while he is awake. He speaks to Joseph while he is asleep. God also spoke to Joseph in an unusual state. Joseph is in the midst of making a tough, life-altering decision. There's no way he fell asleep easily that night. From the moment that Joseph noticed Mary's pregnancy, he must have wondered, "Who's the father?" Here in his dream, God gives Joseph an answer that would shake the world: "I am." God doesn't always speak to us when life is humming along as normal. When we're struggling during a test of faith, we need to pay attention and be ready to obey.

When I was considering planting my current church, I struggled. Did I want to leave a church where I had been for almost twenty years, with a thriving ministry, staff, and facilities? Did I want to put a television ministry I had spent ten years building on the line knowing I might lose it?

These thoughts were racing through my mind as I was sitting in a doctor's office. As I was going back and forward as to what I should do, the thought came to me, *You could stay right where you are and coast the rest of your life.* I picked up a copy of *Forbes* and saw a little quote on the side of the page: "Remember, when you are coasting it is all downhill." I almost looked around to see if God was sitting right beside me speaking into my ear. But I knew God had spoken and I knew God expected me to listen to what he told me and to obey what I heard.

52 Weeks Through the Bible

Are you coasting in life right now? If so, the ride may be fun for a while, but remember that your direction is *down*, not up. The momentum in a Christian's life should always lead us to the next challenge or assignment God has for us. And then when our assignment here on earth is finished, we can look forward to an eternity of being in God's presence.

Don't be in a hurry to take it easy. Listen to what God has next for you. Rarely is it a downhill ride.

28

Demons: The Bad Guys

You believe that there is one God. Good!
Even the demons believe that—and shudder
(JAMES 2:19 NIV).

One of the greatest dangers facing both the church and the world today is not the existence of demons but our disbelief in them…I don't want to underestimate or overestimate the power of demons. Demons do have great power. They give human beings great power. I am often asked, "Is it possible for a Christian to be demon-possessed?" The answer is no. No demon is more powerful than the Holy Spirit. Once the Holy Spirit takes control of a Christian's life, all the demons in hell cannot force him to move out. However, followers of Christ can be demon-influenced. That is why we need to keep our spiritual guard up, stay in the word, continue to pray, and not allow ourselves to fall into temptation.

52 Weeks Through the Bible

The knowledge of God is not what saves us. As James writes, even demons know that God exists. What saves us is an active faith in Jesus Christ as our Savior. That's the kind of faith that not only saves us, but allows us to stand firm against demonic influence. Is there some activity or perhaps upheaval in your life that can be traced to a demonic attack? If so, you *do* have the power to resist that influence and even to put an end to it forever. The same active faith that saves you, also protects you...*if* you use that faith to resist the demonic attack. Don't continue to allow the enemy to influence you in any way. Put an end to it by keeping up your spiritual guard, staying in the word, praying, and walking away from temptation.

29

Angels: The Good Guys

*You have come to Mount Zion, to the city of the living
God, the heavenly Jerusalem.
You have come to thousands upon thousands
of angels in joyful assembly,
to the church of the firstborn,
whose names are written in heaven*
(HEBREWS 12:22-23 NIV).

———

Angels worship, but what may be even more fascinating is that we worship with angels today and they worship with us…From everything we can find in Scripture, angels worshiped God from the time they were created. At almost every great event in the Bible, you will find angels worshiping God. If angels who cannot be saved worship God, how much more should we who have been saved and can have a personal relationship with Christ worship him in spirit and in truth?

52 Weeks Through the Bible

Worship is powerful. Unfortunately, it's often neglected by believers, which is to their loss. Angels know what we should know—that God is to be praised and worshiped at all times, under all circumstances.

How is it with you? Are you rejoicing with the angels today? Have you worshiped? If not, take time now and enter into the angelic chorus giving God his due. It will change your day. And if done daily, worship will change your life.

30

There's More to Life

*The thief does not come except to
steal, and to kill, and to destroy.
I have come that they may have life,
and that they may have it more
abundantly* (JOHN 10:10 NKJV).

The word Jesus uses here for life isn't *bios*, but *zoe*.
Jesus said, "I didn't come just to give you quantita-
tive life. I came to give you qualitative life. There is
more to life than life, and I have come to give you
that more."

As we get older, we get more concerned about the
quality of our life than the quantity of our life. When
we are young, our goal is to have a *long* life. As we
get older, we realize the goal should be a *good* life. As
someone once said, "If I'd known I was going to live
this long, I would have taken better care of myself."

Life is not all about possessions or financial security.
When Jesus called the disciples to follow him, every
one of them left everything behind. Neither did he

guarantee a long or peaceable life; tradition tells us that the disciples died by swords, crucifixion, fire, beheading, or beating.

Because Jesus was God, the life he gives is God-made. It is abundant. It is an overflowing life with surplus and plenty. In Jesus, all our needs are satisfied.

52 Weeks Through the Bible

———————

Most of us live far below God's provision for us. We may have biological life and be content. But Jesus offered us a different kind of life—a life that's superior to biological life. That life, *zoe*, is a gift to us. We don't earn it; we don't have to hunt for it. We only have to ask for it and believe. Never be content with less than what God offers you. Go for the gold. Go for *zoe*.

31

Towel Off

So he got up from the meal, took off his outer clothing,
and wrapped a towel around his waist.
After that, he poured water into a
basin and began to wash
his disciples' feet, drying them with the towel
that was wrapped around him (JOHN 13:4-5 NIV).

Back in that dusty, dirty day of bare feet and sandals, foot washing was a common practice at public baths and upon entering a home. It was the job of a slave, not a self-respecting Jew. In this case, the disciples had rented an upper room, and no slave was present.

To make it clear that he was taking on the role of a slave, Jesus took off his outer clothing, robes that slaves didn't have, and wrapped a towel around his waist just like a slave. Jesus was sending this unmistakable message to his disciples: "Though you know I have all the power, I am surrendering my power and becoming your slave." The One who was higher than the heavens stooped low. The Sovereign of the universe became a servant to his disciples.

When nobody else will take up the towel, a follower of Jesus will. A follower of Jesus will do things other people won't, stand up when others sit, remain silent when others speak, serve when no one else will. As a mom or dad, CEO or manager, captain, teacher, or chief, whatever power, authority, and influence you have, God did not give it to you so you could use it for your benefit. He gave it to you for the benefit of others. A follower of Jesus surrenders his power for the good of others.

52 Weeks Through the Bible

‡

How has God gifted you with talents? Or how has he positioned you to make a difference? Are you available as God's servant? What many Christians miss is the fact that serving others brings great joy to the server. So there should be no sense of drudgery in fulfilling our calling as a servant.

If you are not yet serving, ask God to show you places where you can serve now…or ask him to bring you into a yet-unknown-to-you place where you can serve. When you ask God how or where or who you can serve, he will surely answer. He wants you to experience the joy of serving others.

32

The Warrior Rises

*I will put enmity
between you and the woman,
and between your seed and her Seed;
He shall bruise your head,
and you shall bruise His heel*
(GENESIS 3:15 NKJV).

Before you and I were even born and this world was created, God's Son agreed to become the warrior who would take the sin of the human race upon himself. He would take our punishment, pay the bill, fight the battle, and win the war. It was the way that God could forgive us and still be justified in doing so. Our payment for sin was deferred by God's mercy, demanded by God's justice, but delivered by God's grace.

How do we know he was the warrior promised thousands of years ago in that garden? Because the warrior rises. Many warriors have fought, many warriors have bled, and many warriors have died, but this is the warrior who rises.

You need this warrior. If you try to defeat sin in your own power, you will lose. If you die without this warrior, death wins. Come to the cross and surrender your life to him so that the warrior who rose from the dead will come into your life, fight your battles, and give you victory over sin and life after death.

52 Weeks Through the Bible

———

Many Christians are tired, weary, *exhausted*. They desperately need someone in their corner to help carry the burdens they bear and to fight the battles they're waging. Battles like addictions, financial distress, health issues, broken relationships, fear, anger, and a million other possible conflicts. The good news of the gospel is that we *all* have a warrior on our team. A warrior who has fought in every sort of battle since time began—and never lost one yet.

No matter what your present struggle, call on your warrior, your true hero, your victor. Let him in on the battle. Let him win for you.

Section Six

Church Matters

▸▸▸▸

Jesus promised he would build his church, and beginning in the book of Acts, almost all of the New Testament focuses on its birth, explosive growth, its growing pains, and some of the greatest truths ever penned by human hand. Read and be changed.

52 Weeks Through the Bible

33

Set on Fire!

You will receive power when the
Holy Spirit comes on you;
and you will be my witnesses in Jerusalem,
and in all Judea and Samaria,
and to the ends of the earth (ACTS 1:8 NIV).

Was Jesus's vision too big? Was his mission unreachable? No. In the twentieth century, Christianity became a global faith and is now practiced in large numbers on every continent of the world, particularly Africa, Asia, and South America. Whereas in the early church Christianity was a minority even in Israel, today 90 percent of all Christians live in countries where they are the majority. If we want to be a church ignited by the Holy Spirit, we have a mission to fulfill.

52 Weeks Through the Bible

hy did God give the Holy Spirit to the Christians assembled in the upper room? Why does he give the Spirit to *us*? The answer is the same. The result of having the Holy Spirit invade our lives is that we become witnesses to the saving power of God. The Holy Spirit gave the early Christians boldness to confess their faith before unbelievers. Today, some Christians are hesitant to speak about their faith, even when given the opportunity.

If you have received the Holy Spirit into your life, you *have* received power and you *are* a witness. The work of sharing the good news is not finished. Ask God for the boldness his Holy Spirit inspires. Allow yourself to be used by God to point others to Jesus.

34

Be Sure

I am the way, and the truth, and the life.
No one comes to the Father except
through me (John 14:6).

Contrary to popular assertions, not all religions can and do lead to heaven. If you bypass Christ and you bypass the cross, you bypass heaven…

The cross is both a bridge and a wall. It is a bridge to heaven for those who take it and a wall over heaven for those who reject it. If you are going to become a Christian and be sure that you have eternal life, you must understand that Christ, the only sinless man and Son of God, died for your sins and came back from the dead.

If the world had needed knowledge, God would have sent a teacher. If the world had needed money, God would have sent a philanthropist. If the world had needed technology, God would have sent a scientist. If the world had needed peace, God would have sent a diplomat. But the world needed forgiveness, so God sent a Savior. Forgiveness is the remedy for sin, and when the Savior offers it, we need to receive it. We need to receive him.

52 Weeks Through the Bible

＊＊＊＊

Salvation is in a person, not a philosophy. Not in a code of ethics. Not in a legalistic religious system. Salvation is in Christ alone. When Jesus declared himself as the only way to God, he offended a lot of people back then, and his words still offend a lot of people today.

But truth does that. When we follow the truth—the one who says he is the truth—we too will offend some people. But we are people of the truth. Don't ever hesitate to speak the truth about Jesus. Speak of him to others as their bridge to heaven…or their wall from heaven, whichever they choose. Don't be ashamed of your victor.

35

You Can Know Everything Will Work Out

*We know that God causes all things to work together
for good to those who love God,
to those who are called according to His
purpose* (Romans 8:28 nasb).

If I were to compile a list of the ten most comforting verses in the Bible, Romans 8:28 would make the cut...

The "we" in the first part of the verse refers to those who "love God." This promise is only for those who love God. But this same verse says that these people have been "called according to his purpose." These are the people who have responded to God's call by surrendering to Christ and becoming a child of God. This promise is not for everybody.

What this verse does *not* say is that you will always like or understand what is happening in your life, or that what is happening in your life is always good at the moment. It doesn't say that all things *are* good, but that God causes all things to work together *for good*. God *is* good, and he will make every piece in the puzzle of your life fit perfectly. God doesn't work all things out for our good most of the time or some of the time. God works all things out together for our good all the time.

52 Weeks Through the Bible

—·—·—·—

Every Christian goes through hard times. During that season of adversity, it can be hard to believe that good can come from our situation. From every angle, we see only hopelessness. There is no light at the end of the tunnel. There seems, in fact, to be no end to the tunnel at all.

This is when the suffering Christian truly lives by faith. Will we persist in praising God, even if the situation doesn't right itself for a very long time? Will we trust *no matter what*? The answer can be yes...but our yes can be stronger if decided upon before the adversity hits.

Trust him today and trust him tomorrow. There is an end to your tunnel. There is light awaiting you.

36

The Message That Could Change Your Life

I am not ashamed of the gospel, for it is the power of God for salvation to everyone who believes, to the Jew first and also to the Greek (ROMANS 1:16 NASB).

⬤▬▬▬⬤

The gospel is the most important message you'll ever hear because it's the only one that can and will save your life. The gospel is the only message that has the power to take a person from sin to salvation, from hell to heaven, from deadness to life, and from darkness to light...

Paul got the gospel right, and he went on to say that when you call upon the name of the Lord, if you do it in sincerity and surrender to Jesus Christ, the Holy God *will* save you. Let this verse spark your heart to read through the Bible and understand the gospel. If the gospel is not true, nothing else matters. If true, it is the thing that matters most.

52 Weeks Through the Bible

The word *gospel* literally means "good news." The truth is, the gospel is *great* news. Belief in Christ changes everything. It changes our past by removing all our past sins. It changes our present by giving us power to live boldly every day under any circumstance. It changes our future by guaranteeing us an eternal home—a home that lasts forever and cannot be taken from us. The gospel is the greatest news on earth. Literally.

37

No Small Comfort

Blessed be the God and Father of our Lord Jesus Christ,
the Father of mercies and God of all comfort,
who comforts us in all our affliction,
so that we may be able to comfort
those who are in any affliction,
with the comfort with which we
ourselves are comforted by God
(2 Corinthians 1:3-4).

One of the things I've learned as a pastor is if you talk to anybody long enough and dig deep enough, you discover they have experienced heartache. Each of you reading this sits with a broken heart and broken hopes. Or you know someone who does.

No matter how much you love Jesus and no matter how much you trust God and no matter how faithful you are to his church, you are not immune to horrors and heartaches. The storm of suffering rains on all houses. The wind of hurt blows against all doors.

God never wastes anything. When God created

the universe, there were no leftover stars or planets. There wasn't too much water in the oceans or too much land on the earth. Everything fit perfectly. He will not waste any experience either. When that tragedy strikes, when that heartache comes, when life gives you its worst sucker punch, God's divine counsel is found in his Scriptures...

God is the source of all true comfort. My heart breaks for people who try to find comfort through alcohol, addictions, and abuse—anywhere but God. You can drink yourself, drug yourself, or entertain yourself into a comfortable state, but that comfort won't last. The comfort of God sticks. The comfort of God stands. God himself stays.

52 Weeks Through the Bible

We have a God who *stays*. And in staying with us, he is the source of our comfort. He assures us of his presence, and we have his promise that even this present adversity—this very heartache— he will use to our benefit.

If you're in a place of sorrow, lean hard on God. He is there for you. If your life is running smoothly, rejoice...but then consider that one way God is present with us in adversity is through our brothers and sisters in Christ. Who do you know that is going through a rough patch right now? Can you be the arms and feet of God for that person?

Pray for them, but then call them and ask what they need. Be God's tool.

38

Dying to Live

*I have been crucified with Christ. It is no longer
I who live, but Christ who lives in me.
And the life I now live in the flesh I
live by faith in the Son of God,
who loved me and gave himself for
me* (GALATIANS 2:20).

⊱━━━━⊰

Just as Jesus died for you, when you come to him you die with him. Paul describes what happens in Romans 6:6: "We know that our old self was crucified with him in order that the body of sin might be brought to nothing, so that we would no longer be enslaved to sin."

A Christian should be different because the old you dies and the new you is born. The new you is not just a clone of the old you, a new version put together with the same tired parts. It's all brand-new. Second Corinthians 5:17 says, "Therefore, if anyone is in Christ, he is a new creation. The old has passed away; behold, the new has come."

When people die to self, allowing their desires, preferences, and wants to be crucified and put to death, arguments stop, marriages last, and people start majoring on the majors and forget about the minors.

52 Weeks Through the Bible

――――

What causes most of our heartache in life? Isn't it someone close to us (maybe even ourselves) acting out of fleshly self-interest? Isn't it the uncrucified flesh doing what it does best—thinking first of self?

What would it be like if everyone set aside his or her own interests and considered others as more important? Our lives, families, and nation would be turned upside down—in a good way. We can't change other people, of course. But we can change *us* as we reckon our "old self" dead and ourselves alive to God through our newly created self.

Dying to self is hard. But once we grasp the joy that comes from living entirely by our new creation, we know it's worth hearing the death rattle of our old nature. Don't look at someone else's need to change…just work on yourself. That will be enough to change your world.

39

The Shadow

May I never boast except in the cross
of our Lord Jesus Christ,
through which the world has been crucified to me,
and I to the world (GALATIANS 6:14 NIV).

———◆———

Listen again to these words: "May I never boast except in the cross of our Lord Jesus Christ." The cross doesn't make Jesus special; Jesus makes the cross special. Crucifixion was common in Bible days; over thirty thousand Jews were put to death by crucifixion in the Roman Empire. Jesus experienced a death that thousands of others experienced. But Jesus makes the cross unique because we can live a life every day praising God as a result of it.

The Lord Jesus is God, the Messiah, and the Savior of the world. When you realize who was crucified on that cross and why he was crucified on that cross, then you will live a life of praise.

52 Weeks Through the Bible

When Jesus died on the cross, he didn't die alone. He took us—our old selfish nature—with him. When he died, we died. That sounds like a sad ending…but you know the rest of the story. When he arose from the dead, we arose with him—to newness of life. His resurrection is proof that we are no longer bound to our earthly nature. Now we are risen with him. We are seated with him in heavenly places. We have much to praise God for: Starting with giving us a new resurrection life, continuing on through allowing us to be free from the power of sin, and finally culminating in an eternal home, free from the pains of this life.

40

The Prize Is Not for Sale

*By grace you have been saved through
faith…* (EPHESIANS 2:8).

⸻

Is there a more beautiful word in the entire Bible
than *grace*? Yet, we have the hardest time understanding, giving, and receiving it. Why do humans struggle so much with the idea that salvation and eternal
life are free?

We think everything good, including heaven and
God's presence and pleasure, must be merited. To
think that blessing is something we can earn, deserve,
or achieve by our goodness has been part of idol worship forever. But Paul assures us, "Salvation is not a
reward for the good things we have done, so none of
us can boast about it" (Ephesians 2:9 NLT). Grace is
not only something we cannot earn, but it's given to
people who would never, ever deserve it.

Grace is also hard for us because it messes up our sys-
tems and makes us vulnerable. We love the idea of
winning a prize, but when we're given something by

someone who knows us well, we balk a little. Accepting something that has already been bought and paid for takes all our effort out of the equation. If we receive God's way of salvation as a gift, then we have it. If we try to earn it by our goodness, we will never be able to take it.

Grasping grace is hard because we sometimes want to share the load with Jesus, as if we could climb up on the cross with him. We're treating his death like a down payment if we believe that though he *did* die for our sins, *we* must work to pay the installments. Do you go to church, give money, do good deeds, follow the rules, and somehow believe you're paying for your salvation? Your currency is no good with God.

52 Weeks Through the Bible

When we were children, we liked to "spend" our play money at the pretend grocery store we set up in the garage. That was fun. But if as adults we tried to pay for our groceries with play money, we'd be escorted downtown in a black-and-white car. Play money doesn't buy the real thing.

In the same way, our human efforts at "buying" God's

favor are doomed to fail from the get-go. Oh, yes, God does recognize currency. There is a purchase price for favor with God...but it's a price we couldn't pay...nor do we need to. Christ has paid the bill for us with his blood—the divine currency God recognizes as worthy.

What a rest we enter into when we put away the play money of our human efforts and rely totally on what Christ has purchased for us. No more struggle for acceptance. No more fear of judgment. It's all been paid for. Only foolish pride would reject God's gift to us.

41

One Thing

Brothers, I do not consider that I have made it my own.
But one thing I do… (Philippians 3:13).

━━━━◆━━━━

Many Christ-followers are ineffective in their Christian life and many churches are ineffective in their mission because they are involved in too many things. I can't tell you the number of times people come to me and say, "I would like to serve in our church and go on a mission trip and share my story and be more active, but I've got too many irons in the fire." Sometimes I feel like shouting, "Either pull out some of your irons, or put out the fire!"

Concentration is the secret of power. A river that flows in one direction and one direction only can become a tremendous source of electric energy. If you can take light and concentrate it and its power, you can make a laser that can cut through steel.

The key, then, is to make sure that you set at least one goal that is right. Take a few minutes to think about your goal. What's your *one thing* that will make you productive and pleasing to God and the world?

You might think your *one thing* is too daunting a task. Maybe your *one thing* is to read through the Bible, host a neighborhood barbecue, say yes to a new volunteer role, or rid yourself of an old habit. Be determined just like Paul...Say to yourself, "Today if I don't do anything else, this one thing I will do."

52 Weeks Through the Bible

---

get it when people tell me they're busy. I'm busy too. And the apostle Paul was certainly busy. But despite his full plate, Paul knew what he was called to do. He knew his *one thing*.

What is your one thing? It may be a temporary one thing that will morph into the next one thing in due time, or it might be a lifelong one thing. What's important is that you make room for your one thing by clearing the decks of all your distracting "irons in the fire."

Think about it. Is it time for you to set some things—even *good* things—aside so you can get about your one thing?

42

Rest in Peace

*The peace of God, which transcends all understanding,
will guard your hearts and your minds in
Christ Jesus* (PHILIPPIANS 4:7 NIV).

God's peace, the peace that only God can give, will guard you and protect you from worry and anxiety. It is a peace that passes all understanding because God is the source.

The peace the Bible talks about is not the temporary peace you get through money or drugs or alcohol or sex, because that peace never lasts. This peace transcends understanding. It is so real and so strong that people will look at you and say, "How do you have such peace in the middle of what you are going through?"

You don't have to die to rest in peace. You can rest in peace even when life is at its most difficult. Jesus died not just so we could be forgiven of our sins but so we could have peace in this life. Not just any peace, but peace with God. As Paul says, "Therefore, since we have been justified through faith, we have peace with God through our Lord Jesus Christ" (Romans 5:1 NIV).

When you have peace with God, then you can have the peace of God. No matter what comes your way, you can rejoice, release, and rest in peace.

52 Weeks Through the Bible

We do not live in a peaceful world. If you don't believe me, watch the evening news tonight. And yet in the midst of turmoil—whether worldwide or just in our own small sphere—we can have a supernatural peace that trumps our inclination to worry and fret. God gives us peace, but beyond that, God also has our personal future in his hand at this very moment. How then can we not have peace? We know the God of peace. Let him reign in your heart.

43

More Bang for the Buck

As for the rich in this present age, charge
them not to be haughty,
nor to set their hopes on the uncertainty
of riches, but on God,
who richly provides us with everything to enjoy.
They are to do good, to be rich in
good works, to be generous
and ready to share, thus storing
up treasure for themselves
as a good foundation for the
future, so that they may take
hold of that which is truly life (1 TIMOTHY 6:17-19).

Earthly riches are either going to leave you or you are going to leave them, but eternal riches you keep forever. When you invest in your church, orphanages, missions, clean water, or food and clothing for the poor, you are taking hold of what Paul calls "truly life." True living is found in generous giving.

This is the cycle of generosity: God blesses you today, so you can bless others tomorrow, so he can bless you forever. If you stop the cycle at the beginning, the biggest loser is you because blessings boomerang in the kingdom of God. No matter what you give, how much you give, and how far you give it, God says in eternity it will come back to you many times over.

We all have the opportunity to be generous for the work of the kingdom of God because we know that God's generosity is reflected in our own. "For you know the grace of our Lord Jesus Christ, that though he was rich, yet for your sake he became poor, so that you by his poverty might become rich" (2 Corinthians 8:9). We have eternal riches because Jesus was joyfully generous with us. How can we not with our earthly riches be joyfully generous for him?

52 Weeks Through the Bible

———

Christians are stewards. Spiritually, we're stewards of the gospel. It's our good news to share with those who need Christ. We're also stewards of the material goods God has given us. Just as we share the gospel with the spiritually hungry, so too do we share bread with the physically hungry. We give to ministries that provide food to the poor. Not only our money, but also our time. We give from our wallets, but also from our hands. God has created us to be need-meeters. Watch for God to show you how you can best minister to the needs of others. He will surely show you.

44

The Final Word

*All Scripture is God-breathed and is
useful for teaching, rebuking,
correcting and training in righteousness*
(2 TIMOTHY 3:16 NIV).

The Bible records what God has to say on every
important issue in life—whether it is money, sex,
power, ambition, greed, heaven, or hell. We can
know how to live in a way that pleases God by ascrib-
ing to the Bible's *teaching*.

On the flip side, we need to know what is *not* right,
and the Bible is useful in this *rebuking* way as well.
When you read the Bible, God will speak to your
heart to show you any faults or failures. Like a spiritual CT scan, reading the Bible with an open mind
and an open heart will reveal those wrong thoughts,
attitudes, and habits.

The Bible doesn't just condemn us when we're wrong
and praise us when we're right. It will also show us
what God says we need to do in order to move from

wrong to right. It is useful for *correcting*, for putting us in our proper condition. When you read it and obey it, it restores you to the spiritual condition of being right with God.

The Bible is God's final word to tell you not only what is right and what is not right and how to get right, but you will also hear in it how to stay right. It is profitable for *training in righteousness*.

Every action you take or reaction you experience will either be in line with the will of God or not. The Bible is the final word that helps us not just know the difference but to stay in the place where we can hear from and please and respond to God.

52 Weeks Through the Bible

———

Many a Christian has gone off the rails because they departed from the teaching of Scripture. That's not hard to do in a day when there are so many conflicting philosophies of life available to us. I'm convinced, however, that the wise Christian will not listen to those voices, but instead will follow the voice of the Good Shepherd. Jesus is that Good Shepherd, and by

reading the word, we learn how to live as wise and con-
tented sheep.

Yes, there appears to be green grass just beyond the
safety fence God has given us—but appearances are
deceiving. That "grass" is poisonous to sheep, regardless
of how green it appears. To have true wisdom is to build
our lives on God's word, including receiving correction
and even rebuke when we need it. The Good Shepherd
loves us too much to let us wander without warnings. We
must listen to him.

45

Amazing Grace

The LORD longs to be gracious to you
(ISAIAH 30:18 NIV).

How do you spell salvation? Many people spell salvation D-O. They think one has to do certain actions to be saved—join a church, give to the poor, read the Bible, and pray.

Some people want to spell salvation D-O-N-T. If you don't do certain things, like murder, rape, or steal, then you're saved. But God spells salvation D-O-N-E. No strings attached and no fine print. When you accept Jesus, God accepts you.

The apostle Paul says, "For the grace of God has appeared that offers salvation to all people" (Titus 2:11 NIV). Notice it is not the goodness or religious sincerity of people that brings salvation. It is the grace of God. Grace is an unconditional, unearned, unpurchased, no-strings-attached gift.

Salvation is not based on my performance. It is based on God's promise, not my merit. It is based on God's mercy, not my goodness. Salvation is based on grace.

52 Weeks Through the Bible

————

The truth is if it weren't for grace, no one could be saved. Our sins could never be paid for with any amount of good works we do. That doesn't stop many of us from trying to show God that we merit salvation because of how we live. We have our list of don'ts: We don't murder or steal. We don't cheat. We don't lie.

And our do list is pretty impressive too: We go to church. We put money in the plate. We pray. We treat people nicely. We obey the laws.

And yet neither list—the dos and the dont's—can save us. Only grace can do that. God's wonderful, magnificent, matchless, tremendous grace. It is greater than all our sin.

Section Seven

Curtain Call

———▸▸▸——

The story of the Bible moves toward a curtain call for its hero, Jesus, as he returns for the final time to be acknowledged and acclaimed by the entire world. How should we live as we wait for the hero to return? The Bible has much to teach us about this. Read and be changed.

52 Weeks Through the Bible

46

Breathing Your Last

It is appointed for man to die once,
and after that comes judgment (HEBREWS 9:27).

On a day of God's choosing, not your own, that clock will stop ticking. If you know Jesus, your last breath on earth will be your first breath in heaven. But if you don't know Jesus, your last breath on earth will be your first breath in hell, separated from the God who sent his Son to deliver us from the fear of death and judgment so we could spend eternity with him...

Death is good news for those who believe. At last, we will enjoy the friendship of God, the end of the groaning of creation, a true resurrection life in the loving glory of our Lord, and the death of death once and for all. We will know Christ fully and be known. Breathing your last will mean wholeness, community, and grace.

52 Weeks Through the Bible

Many people are afraid of death. And yet for the Christian, death is truly a beginning, not an end. It's the beginning of a life in the presence of God. A life that will never end. A life with no tears, only joy. Why then should we not accept God's timetable for entrance into heaven?

Here's a way to overcome the fear of death: Commit that future date when you take your last breath into the hands of your heavenly Father. Acknowledge his lordship over your departure from earth. And then stick with it. When the fear of death rears its head, just remember that it's impossible for you to die one second before God allows it. And then ask yourself: Do I really want to live even one day longer than God has planned for me?

47

Root Canal

*See to it that no one fails to obtain the grace of God;
that no "root of bitterness" springs
up and causes trouble,
and by it many become defiled* (HEBREWS 12:15).

A root, like bitterness, is beneath the surface. It is invisible to the eye, but just as real as the plant it supports. A root stretches deep into the soil just as bitterness grows deep into the soil of your heart. Just like roots grow from a seed, so does bitterness. Bitterness is harbored hurt hidden in the heart, so the seed of bitterness is the hurt and the soil of bitterness is the heart.

Our hurt can be inflicted or it can be imagined, but either way the hurt is real. Most hurts are minor enough that we either deal with the hurt or just walk away from it. However, a bitter person doesn't do that. When a bitter person is hurt, he takes that seed of hurt and plants it in his heart. Then he fertilizes it, cultivates it, dwells on it, and then justifies it. All the while, the plant of his life becomes negative and critical of everything attached to his hurt.

Bitterness is a root that we cannot see, but it always bears fruit that we will see. Bitterness finds its root in our heart, but it will bear its fruit in our life. To get to the root of the problem, we must get to our heart.

52 Weeks Through the Bible

Bitterness can destroy a life. It can end relationships, quench our joy, and undermine our relationship with God. There is only one way to overcome bitterness, and that's to go deep into the soil of our heart and pull it by the root. Like a stubborn weed, if we don't get the root, the bitter plant will spring up again.

And how do we remove the root? By learning to forgive. We walk away from assigning blame. We choose to let go. If we need help getting to the root, we can find help in a good Christian counselor.

The worst thing we can do is ignore the root, because we can rest assured it won't ignore us. It will choke out the seeds of joy, peace, and love that God has planted in our hearts. Don't let that happen.

48

The Test of Your Life

Blessed is the one who perseveres under trial because,
having stood the test, that person will receive
the crown of life that the Lord has promised
to those who love him (JAMES 1:12 NIV).

———

A tremendous and almost indescribable blessing awaits at the end of a life that has remained faithful and steadfast in spite of trouble. No matter how deep and hard and heartbreaking the trouble might be, God says to each one of us that if we refuse to buckle and keep believing, trusting, obeying, and serving him, we will receive the crown of life…I don't know what that crown represents, but no earthly reward can compare.

One of the most fascinating and valuable jewels is a pearl. But pearls are the product of pain. The shell of the oyster gets pierced and an alien substance (a grain of sand) slips inside. The sensitive body of that oyster goes to work releasing healing fluids that otherwise would have remained dormant. That irritant is covered and the wound is healed by a pearl. A pearl is a healed wound.

Your life is much the same—conceived through irritation, born in adversity, nursed by adjustments. When all that could be lost is lost and everything that could go wrong does, a person of real faith acts in trust, love, worship, and service, and experiences a future reward of the loving presence of God. Your circumstances right now may be a test, but this test is *for* you.

52 Weeks Through the Bible

When an irritant enters your life, it, of course, doesn't in the least resemble a pearl. It looks more like trouble with a capital *T*. It brings with it emotional pain, possible fear, and even doubts about God. But that irritant (a mild word for it) *is* a pearl at its inception. Pearls are valuable and in just the same way, our trials can be valuable. We need to look past them to the end result—a string of pearls, each born from a different and painful trial. But a trial worth enduring with faith.

49

Faith Works

*As the body apart from the spirit is dead,
so also faith apart from works is dead* (James 2:26).

Faith justifies the believer, but works justify the faith. God sees our faith on the inside, but we demonstrate our faith on the outside. Faith is the root of salvation, but works are the fruit of [salvation]…

You are not saved by Jesus plus baptism. You are not saved by Jesus plus church membership. You are not saved by Jesus plus giving or Jesus plus good works. Jesus doesn't need to add anything and you don't need anything except Jesus in order to know God. Is your faith real? The only way to know it is to show it. If your faith works, you will show it, God will grow it, and others will know it.

52 Weeks Through the Bible

Nobody wants a dead faith. Can a dead faith even save you? James says no. Faith must be walked out in works, not as a means of salvation, but as the fruit of salvation. When Jesus encountered a barren fig tree, he cursed it. That tree was good for nothing if it wasn't going to bear the figs it was created to bring forth.

We were created anew by the Spirit of God to bear fruit. If we are without fruit, what does that say about our so-called faith? Every Christian should seek to have a vibrant, fruitful faith that will cause those around us to notice.

Just remember, fruit is produced by the life within us. Allow the Holy Spirit to bring forth fruit worthy of your salvation.

50

Off-Ramp

*If we say we have no sin, we deceive ourselves,
and the truth is not in us* (1 JOHN 1:8).

Sin is disobeying God or breaking God's law. But when you kneel at the foot of the cross and accept the risen Lord, every sin you have ever committed or ever will commit is forgiven and forgotten by Jesus Christ. The only word found in your legal file is *forgiven*. Guilt will condemn us, but God will clear us. If you're looking for the off-ramp for your guilt trip, take the exit marked "forgiveness."

52 Weeks Through the Bible

Why do so many Christians continue to feel guilty years after their conversion? It has to be because they've never really seen the enormity of their salvation. They must never have really understood grace.

If we have individually knelt at the cross and been forgiven of our sins, we are forever free from the guilt of sin. The only thing that can keep us in guilt are whispers from the enemy ("God can't forgive *that* sin") or unresolved sinful practices that we refuse to take to the cross.

Guilt is a heavy burden no Christian should bear. Forgiven means *forgiven*. And being fully forgiven is the off-ramp from the highway of guilt.

51

Sure Thing

*I write these things to you who believe
in the name of the Son of God,
that you may know that you have
eternal life* (1 John 5:13).

John doesn't say we can think, feel, or hope that we have eternal life; he says *know*. Assurance begins and ends with faith. There are three verbs in verse 13 (*believe*, *know*, *have*), but everything flows from belief. And this verse is in the present tense. It doesn't say, "If you have at one time believed." It says, "If you *now* believe."

The Bible never says that we are right with God because of something we remember in the past, such as getting christened, catechized, or baptized. What matters is not what happened in the past as much as what is happening right now.

I do believe we ought to be able to point to some experience when we realized we were a sinner, that Jesus was the Savior, and we surrendered to him as our Lord. But we don't have to bank on knowing the exact day and time. The great preacher Charles Haddon Spurgeon once said, "A man can know he is alive even if he can't remember his birthday." Thank God that our salvation is not dependent upon a good memory or even a good story.

We are not saved by some past experience. We are saved by our present belief. Being born again is to be made to walk a brand-new life in Jesus. It's a present-tense life with a past-present-future-tense God.

52 Weeks Through the Bible

D o you know beyond the shadow of a doubt that you're a Christian? Have you come to the Father through the Son, Jesus Christ? The apostle John was thinking of you (and all who would read his epistles) when he gave the reason for his letter. He wants you to know that you now have eternal life. This is reality, not a dream. Not a future possibility. Not a maybe. It's a divine *yes*. On this assurance, we find our greatest hope. We are saved for now and eternity.

There is power in knowing we're saved. Though the apostle John wrote this to what he must have thought would be a rather small audience, God meant it for a vast audience—one that spans more than 2000 years. Take John at his word when he tells you to take God at *his* word. If you have trusted Christ, you are a saved person. Period.

52

The Warrior Returns

I saw heaven opened, and behold, a white horse!
The one sitting on it is called Faithful and True,
and in righteousness he judges and
makes war (REVELATION 19:11).

The first two chapters of the Bible introduce us to a utopia called the Garden of Eden. The first man and woman were placed in this pure environment without sickness, suffering, or sorrow—a world no one else has ever seen.

The serpent tempts this first couple to go against the will of God and to disobey the Creator of their perfect world. From that moment until now, the human race has been at war against an enemy it cannot defeat, fighting a battle we're destined to lose.

God's answer to this turmoil is another surprise. He promises to send a warrior. In chapter 32 of this book we learned that this warrior was Jesus, whom God foretold in Genesis 3:15, who was born to a young peasant girl, and who shocked everyone when he died. Just when everyone thought the warrior was dead and the war was lost, there was another surprise—the warrior rises.

His followers took great comfort in the resurrection because the warrior would now finish the task and bring in his kingdom. Nope. Still another surprise. The warrior ascends into heaven, and for over two thousand years, the world is in the same place as before—watching and waiting for the warrior's return…

So the story of the warrior comes to a magnificent close, but those of us who are a part of his army must prepare. We should live now knowing that the warrior is coming. He is coming to bring peace, so we should be peacemakers *now*. He is coming to rule, so we should surrender to him *now*. He is coming to end evil and sin, so we should fight evil *now*. He is coming to eradicate suffering and death, so we should tend to the physical and spiritual needs of others *now*.

The warrior is coming. Will he meet you as friend or foe? I hope as you end this journey you can declare, "Come, Lord Jesus!"

52 Weeks Through the Bible

The Bible is truly a book with a happy ending... a *glorious* ending. And unlike other books with fictional characters who experience the story within the book, we, the readers, get to experience the reality within the book. There will come a day when our great warrior comes again to earth. There will be an end to this present world, but not an end to our lives. How then can we not live for Christ and, if need be, die for Christ? How can we neglect so great a salvation? How can we not tell others of this great true story? How can we not love and help others when they go through hard times?

May God, who has forgiven and forgotten our past, remind us again and again of our future—a future he has lovingly prepared for us. May we keep our eyes peeled for our coming Warrior.

Notes

1. See at http://blog.gideons.org/2010/12/the-bible-contains-the-mind-of-god/.

2. The effort of many to attempt to use the Bible to justify slavery notwithstanding, both William Wilberforce, who is credited for being the catalyst for ending the worldwide practice of slavery, and Martin Luther King Jr, the leader of the American Civil Rights Movement, publicly asserted the Bible as the basis for their leadership and beliefs in these movements. For Wilberforce, see Jonathan Sarfati, "Anti-Slavery Activist William Wilberforce: Christian Hero," Creation.com, February 20, 2007, creation.com/anti-slavery-activist-william-wilberforce-Christian-hero; for King, see David J. Lull, "Remembering Martin Luther King Jr," National Council of Churches of Christ in the USA, www.ncccusa.org/newbtu/lullking.html.

3. John Blanchard, *Is God Past His Sell-By Date?* (Lancaster, PA: Evangelical Press, 2002), 179.

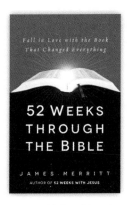

52 Weeks Through the Bible

If you enjoyed *52 Weeks Through the Bible Devotional*, you'll want to read Dr. Merritt's book *52 Weeks Through the Bible*, which takes you on a one-year journey of intimate encounters with God's Word. The simple weekly readings will help you…

- Gain a big-picture view of God's message to you
- Apply practical life lessons from the Bible's stories and teachings
- Discover more about your destiny—on earth and in eternity

As you explore the lives of Israel's wisest kings, God's powerful prophets, and your amazing Savior, you'll see how every subject and story in Scripture paints a picture of God's plan for humanity—including the story God wants to write with *you*.

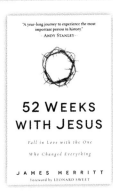

"A year-long journey to experience the most important person in history."
— ANDY STANLEY —

52 WEEKS WITH JESUS

Fall in Love with the One

Who Changed Everything

J A M E S   M E R R I T T

Foreword by LEONARD SWEET

52 Weeks with Jesus

We've heard and seen so many depictions of Jesus that we think we know him better than we do. But if we took the time to really look at him, we might be surprised at what we'd find.

In *52 Weeks with Jesus*, author and pastor James Merritt leads you on a transformative journey as he shares what he's learned over a lifetime of studying Jesus' life and ministry. As you join Dr. Merritt on this journey, you will encounter Jesus in new and surprising ways and be inspired anew to embrace his invitation, "Come, follow me."

Filled with practical applications and surprising truths, this book will help you more ably answer that ancient question that's as timely today as when it was first posed: "Who do you say that I am?"

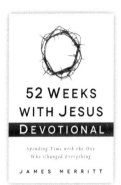

52 Weeks with Jesus Devotional

What difference would it make in your life if you devoted a year to meeting, knowing, and falling in love with Jesus? Dr. James Merritt considered that question, and for 52 weeks, he devoured the Gospels, read books about Jesus, and preached about Jesus from the pulpit.

The result was a change in his life that prompted him to invite others to join him in this profound experience of sitting at the feet of Jesus, absorbing his teaching, his parables, his life. It was a year of humility and grace. A year of removing planks from the eyes. A year of rekindling his passion for Jesus. A year of unparalleled discovery about life itself.

These devotions from that yearlong quest are designed to bring you that same experience of renewal—so that you might have more of Jesus.

About the Author

James Merritt is senior pastor of Cross Pointe Church in Duluth, Georgia, and the host of *Touching Lives*, a television show that broadcasts weekly in all 50 states and 122 countries. He formerly served as a two-term president of the Southern Baptist Convention, America's largest Protestant denomination. As a national voice on faith and leadership, he has been interviewed by *Time*, *Fox News*, *ABC World News*, *MSNBC*, and *60 Minutes*.

He is the author of ten books, including *How to Impact and Influence Others*, *9 Keys to Successful Leadership*, and *9 Ways to Hold on When You Want to Give Up*.

Dr. Merritt holds a bachelor's degree from Stetson University and a master's and doctor of philosophy from Southern Baptist Theological Seminary. He and his wife, Teresa, reside outside of Atlanta near their three children and their grandchildren.

Follow him on Twitter at @DrJamesMerritt.

To learn more about Harvest House books and
to read sample chapters, log on to our website:

www.harvesthousepublishers.com

HARVEST HOUSE PUBLISHERS
EUGENE, OREGON